Ruth

UNDER THE WINGS OF GOD

Other Books by John Piper

A Sweet and Bitter Providence

Velvet Steel

This Momentary Marriage: A Parable of Permanence

Spectacular Sins

When the Darkness Will Not Lift

What Jesus Demands from the World

The Prodigal's Sister

The Innkeeper

The Misery of Job and the Mercy of God

For a complete listing of books by John Piper, see page 92.

Ruth
UNDER THE WINGS OF GOD

JOHN PIPER

Illustrated by
Cory Godbey

:: CROSSWAY

WHEATON, ILLINOIS

Ruth
UNDER THE WINGS
OF GOD

Copyright ©2010 by Desiring God Foundation

Published by Crossway Books
    a publishing ministry of Good News Publishers
    1300 Crescent Street
    Wheaton, Illinois 60187

Cover illustration: Cory Godbey
Cover design: Matt Mantooth

First printing, 2010

Printed in China

Hardcover ISBN: 978-1-4335-1495-1
PDF ISBN: 978-1-4335-1496-8
Mobipocket ISBN: 978-1-4335-1848-5
ePub ISBN: 978-1-4335-1849-2

Library of Congress Catalog-in-Publication Data
Piper, John, 1946-
    Ruth : under the wings of God / John Piper.
       p. cm.
    ISBN 978-1-4335-1495-1 (hc) — ISBN 978-1-4335-1496-8 (pdf)
    1. Ruth (Biblical figure)—Poetry. I. Title.
    PS3566.I59R88 2010
    813' .54—dc22
                                     2009026649

IMG							18	17	16	15	14	13	12	11	10
15	14	13	12	11	10	9	8	7	6	5	4	3	2		

RUTH *Part I*

"My daddy lets me watch three sheep

Beside the mill; and if I keep

Them safe, and make them fat, he said

That next year I'd get five instead.

'If you can keep your three in line,

Then you can handle five at nine.'

My daddy's always making rhymes.

But they're not very good — sometimes."

His grampa laughed. "You're pretty sharp

For being eight. And how's your harp

These days? I'd like to hear you play

Sometime. I heard your daddy say

You've gotten really good. Let's go

Sit down beside the sheep, and show

Me what you've learned." So David took

His grampa down beside the brook

And mill, beneath the carob tree,

And cradled, like a lamb, the C-

Shaped kinnor in his lap and played

A ballad Jews had sung and prayed

For centuries. The old man laid

His head back on the tree and swayed,

As if the music made the tree

A ship mast on the rolling sea.

Then David noticed Obed's eyes

Were closed. "It better satisfies

The ear to close the eye," he once

Had heard his teacher say. "It blunts

The beauty of a thing to feel

A rival pleasure make appeal."

But when he saw on Obed's face

The tears, he stopped. "Grampa, in case

You'd like to hear a happier tune

I know one called 'The Red Raccoon.'

I'm sorry that you're sad. What's wrong?"

"My mother used to play that song."

"You mean Great-grandma Ruth, Grampa?"

"That's right. She was a great grandma

In more ways than you know, young man."

"Grampa, I'd love it, if you can,

To have you tell me all about

Great-grandma Ruth. Can you stay out

With me and tell me how she came

To live in Bethlehem? Her name

Still makes the people smile and sing

Down by the barley fields. They ring

A bell at harvest time, and all

The grown-ups go down every fall

To watch some actors do a play

About Great-grandma Ruth. But they

Won't let the kids go down. It's got

Some parts that Daddy says are not

For kids. Grampa, I am a youth,

But tell me 'bout Great-grandma Ruth."

"The story starts with God, as all

True stories do. As I recall,

Almost a hundred years ago

God stopped the rain and broke the flow

Of blessing in the fruitful land

Of Ephratha. By his command

There was a famine from the shores

Of Lebanon south to the doors

Of Hebron and beyond. And none

Could stay his hand or make undone

The deed of God. He had his aims,

And one of these was Ruth. God names

Whom he will have and moves the earth

To bring them to himself. By birth

She was a Moabite, outside

The Law, and Israel, the bride

Of God, cut off from sacrifice

And priest and covenant. No price

Paid to her gods of wood and stone

Could ever cleanse her heart, atone

For sin, or satisfy the just

And holy claims of God. Sheer dust

Upon the scales, all this, to weigh

Against idolatry each day.

And yet God had a plan to bring

Her out of darkness, make her cling

To him, and give her royal seed."

"Grampa, what's royal seed?" "A breed

Of children, David, who will be

Like kings. I don't know how. But she

Was sure and prophesied. We need

It too. But let's go back. What deed

Delivered her out of the hand

Of Chemosh, brought her to the land

Of Israel, and put her name

In songs and gave her godly fame?

It was a famine, David. God

Closed up the clouds and laid his rod

Against the back of Israel."

"But, Grampa, how did famine tell

Great-grandma Ruth to leave her land

And come to Bethlehem?" "The hand

Of God is very roundabout,

And there is time and room to doubt

At every turn, my son. A man

Of Bethlehem was in the plan.

His name: Elimelech. He took

His wife Naomi and forsook

The land of God. It was an act

Of unbelief. Naomi packed,

But every movement was a grief.

She knew that God would bring relief

If they would stay in Israel,

If they would seek his face and dwell

Among the righteous few who cleave

To future grace. 'But that's naive,'

Elimelech replied. 'There's grain

In Kedemoth, but only pain

In Bethlehem.' And so they went,

Unknowingly, to judgment sent,

But also on an errand of

Amazing grace and sovereign love."

"You mean, Grampa, because they'd find

Great-grandma Ruth?" "That's right. But mind

You, David, this was all of God.

None saw the wielding of the rod

To save the tail and strike the head.

One year, Elimelech was dead.

And then the rebel sons, to break

Naomi's heart, began to take

In Moab girls." "What do you mean,

Grampa?" "I mean, young man, that clean

And upright boys will never sleep

With girls until the day they keep

One woman for a wife. Beware,

Young man, no commoners should dare,

Nor even kings, to break this law.

Naomi trembled at the raw

And lustful sins of Chilion.

And Mahlon would carouse till dawn.

'No more!' she cried. 'I meant for you

To have two virgin wives. And do

You plan to put me in the grave

Beneath this soil, or in a cave

Cut for a Moabite?' And so

To mock their mother's faith, as though

To grant her holy wish, they sought

Two virgin Moabites, and bought

Them with the birthright of their dad."

"Wow, Grampa, they were really bad."

"But, David, do you know who those

Wives were whom these blind rebels chose?

One's name was Orpah, here's the truth:

The other was Great-grandma Ruth."

"But, Grampa, that sounds terrible."

"Oh, no, my lad, incredible

Is what it was. The rescue of

The century: relentless love

Is what it was. The broken saint

Just took them in without complaint,

And from her lips and from her way

They met her God and learned to pray.

And then one day, as quickly as

Their dad, her sons were dead. It has

The ring of judgment, David. Do

You see? They drowned while swimming through

The Arnon River just to spite

The bragging of a Moabite.

Naomi wept till she could weep

No more, and then she said, 'I sweep

My place today, tomorrow I

Will leave it clean, and by and by,

God helping me, I'll put my feet

In Bethlehem, and there complete

My years with bitter memories.

Go back and find your families.

I have no sons to offer now,

Nor any man to keep his vow.

The Lord be with you in the house

Where you grew up, and may your spouse

Be better than the last.' And so

She kissed Orpah farewell. 'Now go.'

But when she turned to Ruth, she saw

A different face. As if the Law

Of God, with every promised hope

And all of its eternal scope

Were written on her very soul

Unrolling like an endless scroll.

And thus she spoke: 'Entreat me not,

That I return, or take my lot

Again among the Moabites

With wooden gods and pagan rites.

Turn me not back to these, but let

Me go with you. Whatever threat

Or hope you have, I will embrace.

I have no other dream or place

To live. Where you stay, I will stay.

The path you take will be my way.

And where you die, there I will die,

And bury me beneath the sky

Of Israel. There is a call

Upon my life, Naomi. All

That you've endured these ten long years

Has been for me and you. And tears

Cannot conceal that offspring yet

To come through us will not forget

To praise the bitter providence

Of God that wrought for us immense

And precious mercies in this place

And lavished me with painful grace.

A rod of famine was the price

For me that opened paradise.

I am a Moabite to you,

But more than that, your daughter too.

Come, let us leave this place, I cleave

To you, Naomi. I believe,

Beneath this sweet and bitter rod,

That your great God will be my God.'"

"Grampa, how did you memorize

All that?" "It came with lullabies

And ballads that she sang to me,

Just like the one you played. Could be,

My good grandson, that you will sing

Like that and put the truth on wing

With harp and psalm and song. She would

Be pleased. Perhaps, then, if you should,

Your son, when you are gone someday,

Will sing it in a whole new way."

And so with faithful Ruth we pray

That bitter providence today

Tomorrow will taste very sweet,

And every famine that we meet

And every broken staff of bread

In death, will bring us life instead.

RUTH *Part II*

"Grampa, when I put my three sheep

Down in the fold tonight to sleep,

Can you stay here and tell me more

About Great-grandma Ruth before

I go to bed? Naomi said,

Because Elimelech was dead,

And both her sons, that when

She came to Bethlehem again,

There would be bitter memories

For her and nothing more. Are these

The only things, Grampa, that she

Could see? Just grief? It seems to me

That God was doing more." "Indeed

He was. But, David, sometimes creed

Can't keep up with the speed of pain

And has to make the meaning plain

When suffering slows down. Do you

Know what I mean?" "I think it's too

Complex, Grampa." "I mean that what

Naomi knew of God was not

Rejected when she wept her way

Back home to Bethlehem. The day

Would come when tortoise faith would catch

The bounding hare of pain and match

His power, not his pace, and win.

Judge not from how the two begin.

Does that make sense?" "I think it does.

But, Grampa, tell me what it was

That turned it all around and made

Naomi glad again."

"She prayed.

And, David, when she prayed, God did

A hundred miracles and bid

A barley field become a place

Of quiet pow'r; and there the race

Of faith was won. My dad, your great-

Grandfather, Boaz, conquered hate

And loved a Moabite beneath

The wings of God and did bequeath

Naomi, thus, more faith than she

Had ever known or thought could be."

"Oh, Grampa, that's the part that most

Of all I'd like to hear. I'll post

The gate and put the sheep away

And you can eat with us, okay?"

"I have a better plan. You get

Permission from your dad to let

You spend the night with me, and we

Will go down to my house and see

The very place, the barley field,

Where, seven decades past, God sealed

A kind of love that's known by few:

Between a Moabite and Jew.

And, David, did you know that your

Great-grampa Boaz has a pure

And faithful memory of what

It cost him then? There's yet a lot

Of love, though he turns ninety-nine

This year and cannot see. But line

On line, he knows the story of

His Ruth and how they came to love

Each other when the barley yield

Was ripe and they met in the field.

I think you're old enough to go

And visit him. But he won't know

Your name or who you are. So bring

Your harp, and maybe we can sing

Our way into his mind and set

Some memory on wing, and get

The treasure of his heart up to

His lips."

       At dusk the east wind blew,

And as the sun was going down,

The two approached the little town

Of Bethlehem and made their way

Around the soft and splashing bay

Of blowing barley waves. The house

Was small, for neither had a spouse.

"A servant boy and two old men

Can manage with a fox's den,"

Old Obed used to say when folks

Would pester him and try to coax

The two of them to live at home

With Jesse's family. "I roam

The local hills at my own pace,"

He said, "and come back to my place."

Tonight Boaz was by the fire

And wrapped in blankets for attire.

Young David stood in awe that here

Was his own flesh who, in a year,

Would have a century of life

Perhaps, on earth and one whose wife

Was his Great-grandma Ruth. He took

His harp and cradled in the crook

Of his small arm the music of

A fam'ly's century of love.

When Boaz heard the song that he

And Ruth had sung for sixty-three

Unbroken years, he blinked his blind

And glassy eyes. And then a kind

Of deep and strong and gentle joy

Began to shine. "Come here, my boy,"

He whispered. David stopped and sat

Down at the old man's feet. "Is that

A story you would like to know?"

He asked. "How Boaz, long ago,

Became the husband of a maid

From Moab, even though he swayed

A city with his wealth?" "Yes, sir,

I would. Why did you marry her?"

"It wasn't easy, child, at least

For some. A woman from the east,

And not a Jew, was barely good

Enough to be a slave and would

Not enter any mind to be

A wife. My father couldn't see

What I could see. I still recall

His bitter speech: 'Boaz, the gall,

To bring this on our family!

The girl's a Moabite, and she

Has got no name. She was a slave,

And Mahlon was a rebel knave

To buy her as a virgin just

To pique his mother and his lust.

And don't you know, Boaz, the way

Her people got their start? Don't say

It was a noble thing that Lot

Was drunk and lay down on his cot

With his own daughter. She deceived

Her grieving father and conceived

A child by incest. And his name?

Moab! A people born in shame.

And, Boaz, will you sacrifice

Your name — our name — and, by that price,

Raise up a sinful seed, and on

My head heap shame when I am gone?

And while I live will you disgrace

My silver head and go abase

Yourself to marry such a thing?

And even use your mother's ring?'"

He paused, as if the sting were yet

Alive. "I never will forget

Those words." "Great-grampa, how did you

Reply?" "I said to him, 'It's true

That she's a Moabite and that

Her husband was apostate at

The core and that she was a slave

And has no high-born name to save

From stigma and contempt. And should

The sin of Lot destroy the good

For every generation, then

There is no good in any men.

I bid you, father, think with care,

Lest you forget the evil pair,

Five generations past, that bore

Our father Perez at the door

Of harlotry. Incest is not

Unique to Moabites. We got

Our life from Tamar's little trick

To get the seed of Judah. Pick

Your people, tongue, or tribe, for none

Is pure from disrepute, not one.

But, Father, have you thought about

What Ruth is like inside? I doubt

That in a thousand Israelites

One has embraced our God with heights

Of faith one-half as free and great

As she. Do you desire a mate

For me with Jewish nose and skin,

Or sacred Jewish faith within?

And is there not more fruit in her

Than can be hidden with a slur?

For those who care about the truth

There is none fairer than my Ruth.

They all can see her love for God,

How she has borne the biting rod,

And loved Naomi without pay,

And worked throughout the blist'ring day,

And gathered only where the poor

May glean, and kept her garments pure

Among the men. This woman lives

Beneath the wings of God. It gives

Me more delight to share the shame

Of faith and love than save my name.

I love you, Father, and I pray,

Please look at her another way.'"

"Grampa, I mean, Great-grampa, sir . . ."

"Yes, son?" "I'm glad you married her."

"Me too. I think I better sleep

Now, son. I'm sure the rest will keep

Until tomorrow. So despite

How much more I could say, good night."

And meanwhile in the darkness here,

Where tribes and races hate and fear,

O Lord, grant that we now ignite

A flame of truth, and let us fight

With love and joy to make it plain

That fam'ly links are not a chain,

And origins do not control;

Half-images are not the whole,

Nor true, and take a rending toll;

Beneath the skin there is a soul.

And may we lift this light and truth

For Boaz and for ev'ry Ruth.

RUTH *Part III*

When David woke, he was surprised

To see old Boaz energized,

And waiting for the boy to wake.

The old man couldn't see or make

His feet tread where his mind said, Go.

But he could recollect, and, Oh,

How he did love to tell the tale

Of how the God of Israel

Turned famine into wedding feast,

And formed the greatest from the least,

And wakened love when it had died,

And brought a Moabitess bride

Into his life, and made a field

Of barley, barren once, to yield

Such seed as he had never dreamed.

He heard the boy awake and beamed,

"Young man, my son tells me that you

Are David, Jesse's son." "That's true,

And you're my great-grampa." "Last night

I didn't know, without my sight,

That it was you. Come here and let

Me touch your face. There is a debt

To parentage that one can feel.

My wrinkled fingers can reveal

More memories of Ruth than both

My eyes. Yes, there, a little growth,

And that will be her nose, and this,

Her cheek, where once I placed my kiss.

Obed!" "Yes, Father?" "Take me and

The boy down by the gleaning stand.

You know the one." So Obed took

His father in his arms. A look

Told David to make wide the door.

He set him on a cart before

The cottage plot, and then the three

Of them, at dawn, rode happily

Down to the gleaning stand. The face

Of Boaz beamed as if the place

Were like a home, and he had been

Away for years. And Obed's grin

Burst into laughter once or twice,

As if he drove to paradise.

It was a bright and lucid dawn,

And both of these old men were drawn

Not just by this well-seasoned mare,

But by a memory out there

Beyond the edge of Bethlehem,

Where bitter providence for them

Had been reversed, and God had turned

A famine into feast. It burned

Inside their happy hearts with hope,

And as they rode the final slope

Down to the gleaning stand, the two

Old Israelites, one blind and due

In heaven thirty years ago,

The other one with hair like snow,

Broke into song.

"O barley field! O barley field!

When you were bent with heads,

I feasted on your ample yield

And ate your simple breads.

O barley field! O barley field!

All scorched with desert breath,

You starved the one I would have healed

And stole my love in death.

O barley field! O barley field!

A paradise in truth,

You kept for me a better yield

And brought to me my Ruth."

"Great-grampa, you

Made up that song. But tell me who

You mean — the one you would have healed

But lost in death." The wagon wheeled

Down to the gleaning stand and stopped.

The morning sun warmed all, and topped

The half-grown grain with tiny crowns

Of gold, and wrapped the trees in gowns

Of yellow green. "Yes, David, I

Will answer you. But first now, try

To put yourself back eighty years.

Your grampa isn't born. Great fears

Grip all of Judah. Drought has left

The barley field unsown, bereft

Of even root and stem. I'm not

Quite nineteen years of age. This spot,

One year ago at seventeen,

I married Mara." "Do you mean,

Great-grampa, you were married once

Before?" "I was, for fourteen months.

Eight weeks before she died, again

Here at the gleaning stand, the men

Persuaded me to leave and go

With them to Moab. I should show,

They said, my bride more love and take

Her to a place where there is cake

And wine. But when I told her of

The plan, she said, 'Boaz, such love,

You know full well, will not endear

Me to your soul. In this I hear

The counsel of Elimelech,

Your uncle. And I will not trek

To Moab in his godless train.

It is not love to trade for grain

Your God. I will not suck with these

The breast of foreign deities.

I'd rather starve beneath the wings

Of God than live with foreign kings.'

And so we stayed. Eight weeks, and she

Was dead — too weak and thin to see

The fever through. And as she died

She said, 'Our God is on your side,

Boaz, and do not doubt that this

Is best. I know there is more bliss

In dying underneath the wings

Of God than living by the springs

Of Chemosh. Boaz . . .' 'Yes, I'm here.'

'Boaz, I don't want you to fear.

I had a priceless dream last night.

I dreamed that God would show his might

And take your bitter providence

And by this famine here dispense

For you a feast — a wedding feast —

And make the greatest of the least,

And waken love when it has died,

And bring an unfamiliar bride

Into your life, and make this field

Of barley, barren once, to yield

Such seed as you have never dreamed.

And that he will be born esteemed

In this our little town, so small

Among the clans, and God will call

Him out of ancient days to sway

The nations with his rod. Don't say

That you were wrong. This very hour

God makes the sin of man, with power,

To serve your faithfulness. In ten

Short years you will be healed. And then . . .'

'Oh, Mara, what of you?' 'My task

Is done. The Lord did only ask

That I should serve to keep you here,

Lest out of mingled love and fear

You flee to Moab and make void

The mercy of your God. Employed

For such a God-like work, your bride

Is now content to step aside.'

And ten years later, David, there,

Just there beside the stand, as fair

As any in the world, stood Ruth.

She rested in the gleaners' booth.

Ten years to turn the mutiny

Of sin into the ecstasy

Of faith. I knew that it was she

I watched her, breathless, steadily.

I still can see her tawny neck.

The daughter of Elimelech!

Do you see, David, why we sing?

O barley field! O barley field!

A paradise in truth

You kept for me a better yield

And brought to me my Ruth.

I'd rather live beneath the wing

Of God, or die there if I must,

Than try to save my life by trust

In my own plans. Oh, David, do

You understand? O son, how few

There are who wait for God to act!

How few who trust the solid pact

That God has made, that he will work

For those who wait for him, nor shirk

One moment in a ten-year plan,

Or more. Perhaps he wills to span

A thousand years before the space

Of time is full for him to place

His final king upon the throne.

And when he does, it shall be known

That here in Bethlehem we played

A part.

  If you are not afraid,

Tonight, God willing, we will ride

Down here again, and I will guide

You to the place that I love best

And sightless show you all the rest.

So waiting is a holy work

Of faith in God. Nor does there lurk

Beneath the timing of his ways

Some secret malice that displays

Itself in holding back the flow

Of future grace. God does not go

From here to there by shortest routes;

He makes a place for faith and doubts.

Nor does he hasten on his way,

But comes when it is best, today,

Or maybe twenty years from now,

Or more. With Boaz we will bow

To God, and there embrace the truth:

Some serve like Mara, others Ruth.

RUTH *Part IV*

Now blind and lame, the old man drew

The blanket close and clutched the shoe

That he held in his lap and sat

Beside his faithful son. And at

The back the boy rode bumping down

The same hill from the quiet town

Of Bethlehem. The wooden cart

Was witness to the master art

Of Obed's craft. When he was ten

He built it for the poorest men

And women who would glean the sheaves

That every godly farmer leaves

In Judah for the ones who own

No land. His mother, Ruth, had shown

Him how she used to gather grain

And beat it out, and what a strain

It was to take the winnowed seed

And walk it up the hill. "They need

A cart," she said. "Don't you believe,

My son, that Moses meant to weave

Together with his law that we

Leave something for the poor, a plea

That, if we can, we help them bear

It up the hill and take it where

They need to go? It seems to me

The holy Torah ought to be

Interpreted to see as much

Compassion as we can. The touch

Of heaven's love from this great Book

Once wakened me from death and shook

Me to the bottom of my soul.

Why not make something that can roll,

And let the gleaners use it when

They're tired?" And so the boy, at ten,

Built them a cart. He thought, "Perhaps

My cart, made out of love and scraps,

Will help the poor to see the hand

Of God and trust in what he's planned."

Now sixty years have passed. Tonight

The aged craftsman drives his bright

And eager grandson and his blind

And failing father down to find

The place he promised David they

Would go when it was dark. The gray

Of twilight turned to night. The boy

Could see on Boaz' face a joy

That broadened to a wrinkled smile.

He knew the ruts of every mile,

Especially the final two

Around the fields, that led down through

The hollow where he used to sift

The barley seed at night and lift

The spirits of his workers there.

He used to sing a song, and wear

The same clothes as the working men,

And rake and toss his share. And when

The other owners asked him why,

He said, "The Torah says that I

Should love my neighbor just the way

I love myself. Would you not say

That if you labored for a boss,

It would be good to see him toss

The barley every now and then?

We ought to read the Torah, men,

To see as much compassion as

We can. Go read, and find it has

More mercy than you think." But these

Were not the only memories

That made the old man smile tonight.

"Stop here, Obed," he said. "The light.

How much is there tonight? Is there

A moon? And are there stars?" "It's fair,

My father, and the moon is full."

"That's good," he said, "Obed, let's pull

The cart down to the cedar at

The end." "Great-grampa, isn't that

The one where all the people go

To watch the play?" He laughed. "You know

About the play?" "I don't know much.

They say it's all about the touch

Between you and Great-grandma Ruth."

"This is my favorite spot," the old

Man said, "And now you shall be told

About that touch and where it led.

Here seventy short years have sped

Away since that great night. Because

The heat was great by day, I was

Down winnowing at dark. And when

The work was done, I told the men

To fetch the food and wine so we

Could eat and rest. I couldn't see

What God was just about to do.

When I was full and tired, I threw

This blanket over me and lay

Down underneath that tree. Today

It must be twice as big. I fell

Asleep and dreamed about my belle."

"You mean Great-grandma Ruth?" "I do.

And, David, then my dream came true.

At midnight something stirred beneath

My blanket at my feet. My teeth

Clamped like a vise. I carefully

Unsheathed my knife and tried to see

Where I could strike the beast to kill,

Lest I should miss the head, and still

Be bitten by some snake or worse,

I knew not what. It is a curse,

I thought, for dreaming of my Ruth.

And as I raised the knife, the truth

Rose like a hand against my wrist.

I looked and thought, 'This moonlit twist

Beneath the blanket at my feet

Is not a snake. Nor will it eat

My leg. This is a human form.

A child in search of being warm

Perhaps. Or worse, some woman of

The street who hopes to sell me love.'

I whispered, so as not to wake

The men, 'Who are you? Do not make

A sudden move or you will die.

If you're a child and cannot buy,

You shall be fed. But if a wench,

You will find nothing here, nor quench

Your hunger in my bed. I would

Not touch a woman, be she good

Or great, outside a covenant,

Though there is one I truly want.'

I pulled the blanket gently back

And there, as still as night, the black

And piercing eyes of Ruth. 'My name

Is Ruth,' she said. 'Your servant came

Because Naomi told me I

Should lie down at your feet and by

This action say you are a kin

To her, in hope that she may win

Your willingness to raise up seed

To Mahlon, if you are agreed.'

'These are Naomi's words, I hear.

I know her mind, but not, I fear,

Her daughter's heart. This too I would

Be pleased to learn. I hope you could,

Besides this well-taught speech, reveal

Your own designs and how you feel

About the prospect in her mind.

Have you emotions unassigned?'
She lay there motionless, then said,
'My heart's desire is that you spread
Your holy wing and cover me.'"

"Great-grampa Boaz, I don't see
What all this means." "Well, David, now
You know why they do not allow
The kids to come down to the play
Each year. But listen, here's the way
It ends. My heart was beating in
My throat, and crouching there was sin,
Awaiting one misstep. I spoke
The hardest words and almost broke:
'There is another kinsman still

More close to you than I. He will

Be given legal right to take

You if he will. Tomorrow make

Your prayer, and I will settle this

With elders in the gate.' No kiss

That night. But when she left, still dark,

She took my hand and drew an arc

And said, 'The God of Exodus

And flood at dawn will fight for us.'

That was our only touch.

And so

As soon as light shone on the low

Gate leading into Bethlehem

I gathered elders and to them

Laid out my case, and to the head

Whose right preceded mine I said,

'Naomi's land is yours. The claim?

You marry Ruth, and keep the name

Of Mahlon in your line. Declare

Your will, for I am next, and swear

That I will take her if you can't.'

I wondered how the Lord would grant

The longing of my heart and by

Another providence comply

With Ruth's appeal and my desire.

And then I learned. He said, 'Acquire

It for yourself. The land I would

Have had, for it is very good.

But Ruth? She is a Moabite,

And we are Jews. It isn't right.

The land is yours, and Mahlon's name

For what it's worth. And Ruth. And shame.'

He took his shoe and gave it to

Me in the gate. I turned and threw

It out to Ruth among the crowd.

She caught it like a wreath and bowed.

I quieted the shouts and cried,

'What do you think of this, my bride?'

And she replied, 'I think the Lord

Has fought today and with his sword

Has stuck a sin up on the gate

And hung on it our wedding date.

As for the badge of shame, you tell:

The line of Judah bears it well,

And will for generations yet

To come. The book of Moses set

Me free. There is a mercy in

The law of God beyond my skin:

By faith God makes a person right,

Be she a Jew or Moabite.'"

O God, she was a rock of truth;

Ignite in us the faith of Ruth.

COMPLETE LIST OF BOOKS BY JOHN PIPER

God's Passion for His Glory

The Pleasures of God

Desiring God

The Dangerous Duty of Delight

Future Grace

A Hunger for God

Let the Nations Be Glad!

A Godward Life

Pierced by the Word

Seeing and Savoring Jesus Christ

The Misery of Job and the Mercy of God

The Innkeeper

The Prodigal's Sister

Recovering Biblical Manhood and Womanhood

What's the Difference?

The Justification of God

Counted Righteous in Christ

Brothers, We Are Not Professionals

The Supremacy of God in Preaching

Beyond the Bounds (with Justin Taylor)

Don't Waste Your Life

The Passion of Jesus Christ

Life as a Vapor

A God-Entranced Vision of All Things (with Justin Taylor)

When I Don't Desire God

Sex and the Supremacy of Christ (with Justin Taylor)

Taste and See

Fifty Reasons Why Jesus Came to Die

God Is the Gospel

What Jesus Demands from the World

Amazing Grace in the Life of William Wilberforce

Battling Unbelief

Suffering and the Sovereignty of God (with Justin Taylor)

50 Crucial Questions

When the Darkness Will Not Lift

The Future of Justification

The Supremacy of Christ in a Postmodern World (with Justin Taylor)

Spectacular Sins

Finally Alive: What Happens When We Are Born Again

John Calvin and His Passion for the Majesty of God

Rethinking Retirement

This Momentary Marriage: A Parable of Permanence

Stand: A Call for the Endurance of the Saints (with Justin Taylor)

Velvet Steel

A Sweet and Bitter Providence

THE SWANS ARE NOT SILENT SERIES

The Legacy of Sovereign Joy

The Hidden Smile of God

The Roots of Endurance

Contending for Our All

Filling up the Afflictions of Christ

⚙ desiringGod

If you would like to further explore the vision of God and life presented in this book, we at Desiring God would love to serve you. We have hundreds of resources to help you grow in your passion for Jesus Christ and help you spread that passion to others. At our website, desiringGod.org, you'll find almost everything John Piper has written and preached, including more than thirty books. We've made over twenty-five years of his sermons available free online for you to read, listen to, download, and in some cases watch.

In addition, you can access hundreds of articles, find out where John Piper is speaking, learn about our conferences, discover our God-centered children's curricula, and browse our online store. John Piper receives no royalties from the books he writes and no compensation from Desiring God. The funds are all reinvested into our gospel-spreading efforts. Desiring God also has a whatever-you-can-afford policy, designed for individuals with limited discretionary funds. If you'd like more information about this policy, please contact us at the address or phone number below. We exist to help you treasure Jesus Christ and his gospel above all things because he is most glorified in you when you are most satisfied in him. Let us know how we can serve you!

Desiring God
Post Office Box 2901
Minneapolis, Minnesota 55402
888.346.4700
mail@desiringGod.org
www.desiringGod.org